HeadStart
primary

SPELLING
YEAR 4

Written by Clive Stack

Acknowledgements:

Author: Clive Stack
Series Editor: Peter Sumner
Illustration and Page Design: Cliff Woodcock and Jerry Fowler

The right of Clive Stack to be identified as the author of this publication has been asserted by him in accordance with the Copyright, Designs and Patents Act 1998.

HeadStart
primary

HeadStart Primary Ltd
Elker Lane
Clitheroe
BB7 9HZ

T. 01200 423405
E. info@headstartprimary.com
www.headstartprimary.com

All rights reserved. No part of this publication may be reproduced, stored in a retrieval system, or transmitted in any form or by any means, electronic, mechanical, photocopying, recording or otherwise without the prior permission of the publisher.

Published by HeadStart Primary Ltd 2018 © HeadStart Primary Ltd 2018

A record for this book is available from the British Library -
ISBN: ISBN 978-1-908767-66-0

Year 4

CONTENTS

Twiggy
Buddy
Blossom
Bean
Petal
Sprout

Teachers' Notes	i – ix
Spelling Overview	x – xii
Practice Sheets	
Term 1 (Sets 1, 2, and 3)	1 – 12
Term 2 (Sets 1, 2, and 3)	13 – 24
Term 3 (Sets 1, 2, and 3)	25 – 35
Activity Sheets	
Term 1 Set 1	36 – 43
Term 1 Set 2	44 – 51
Term 1 Set 3	52 – 59
Term 2 Set 1	60 – 67
Term 2 Set 2	68 – 75
Term 2 Set 3	76 – 83
Term 3 Set 1	84 – 91
Term 3 Set 2	92 – 99
Term 3 Set 3	100 – 105
Spelling Tests	
Teachers' Scripts	106 – 113
End of Term Test: Term 1	114
End of Term Test: Term 2	115
End of Term Test: Term 3	116
End of Year Spelling Test (1)	117
End of Year Spelling Test (2)	118
Pupils' Answer Sheet	119
Teachers' Record Sheet	120
Additional Material	
Themed Spelling Lists	121 – 127
Spelling Games and Grids	128 – 135
Blank Practice Sheet	
S P U D Poster	

SPELLING YEAR 4

HeadStart primary

SPELLING • YEAR 4

Practice Sheet

Term 1 Set 1 Week 1

Name .... Date ....

Spelling patterns adding suffixes to words of more than one syllable, **extension**, word list

I've never regretted my decision limiting my TV time.

Spellings	Write	Write	Cover and write	Cover and write
regret	regret	regret	regret	regret
regretting	regretting	regretting	regretting	regretting
regretted	regretted	regretted	regretted	regretted
limit	limit	limit	limit	limit
limiting	limiting	limiting	limiting	limiting
limited	limited	limited	limited	limited
occurrence	occurrence	occurrence	occurrence	occurrence
budgeted	budgeted	budgeted	budgeted	budgeted
accidentally	accidentally	accidentally	accidentally	accidentally
actually	actually	actually	actually	actually

✓ ✓ ✓ ✓ ✓ ✓ ✓ ✓ ✓ ✓

Checked

Total 10 /10

SPELLING YEAR 4

© Copyright HeadStart Primary Ltd

Practice Sheet

Term 1 Set 1 Week 2

Name .... Date ....

Spelling patterns adding suffixes to words of more than one syllable, **extension**, word list

> I don't deny it! I'm a committed and determined fidgeter.

Spellings	Write	Write	Cover and write	Cover and write
commit	commit	commit	commit	commit
committing	committing	committing	committing	committing
committed	committed	committed	committed	committed
fidget	fidget	fidget	fidget	fidget
fidgeting	fidgeting	fidgeting	fidgeting	fidgeting
fidgeted	fidgeted	fidgeted	fidgeted	fidgeted
regrettable	regrettable	regrettable	regrettable	regrettable
benefitted	benefitted	benefitted	benefitted	benefitted
believe	believe	believe	believe	believe
bicycle	bicycle	bicycle	bicycle	bicycle

Total /10

Practice Sheet

Term 1 Set 1 Week 3

Name .... Date ....

Spelling patterns adding suffixes to words of more than one syllable, **extension**, word list

My seat belt was fast<u>ened</u> so tightly I could hardly breath<u>e</u>.

Spellings	Write	Write	Cover and write	Cover and write
refer	refer	refer	refer	refer
referring	referring	referring	referring	referring
referred	referred	referred	referred	referred
fasten	fasten	fasten	fasten	fasten
fastening	fastening	fastening	fastening	fastening
fastened	fastened	fastened	fastened	fastened
forgettable	forgettable	forgettable	forgettable	forgettable
focused	focused	focused	focused	focused
breathe	breathe	breathe	breathe	breathe
business	business	business	business	business

marked

Total 10 /10

SPELLING YEAR 4

© Copyright HeadStart Primary Ltd

Practice Sheet

Term 1 Set 1 Week 4

Name .... Date ....

Spelling patterns adding suffixes to words of more than one syllable, **extension**, word list

Are you admitting you've been caught red-handed?

Spellings	Write	Write	Cover and write	Cover and write
admit	admit	admit	admit	admit
admitting	admitting	admitting	admitting	admitting
admitted	admitted	admitted	admitted	admitted
offer	offer	offer	offer	offer
offering	offering	offering	offering	offering
offered	offered	offered	offered	offered
forbidden	forbidden	forbidden	forbidden	forbidden
preference	preference	preference	preference	preference
caught	caught	caught	caught	caught
century	century	century	century	century

Total 8 /10

SPELLING YEAR 4

© Copyright HeadStart Primary Ltd

Practice Sheet

Term 1 Set 2 Week 5

Name .... Date ....

Spelling patterns the prefixes **il-, im-, ir-, extension**, word list

Certain irregular verbs are very difficult to spell.

Spellings	Write	Write	Cover and write	Cover and write
legal	legal	legal	legal	legal
illegal	illegal	illegal	illegal	illegal
mature	mature	mature	mature	mature
immature	immature	immature	immature	immature
regular	regular	regular	regular	regular
irregular	irregular	irregular	irregular	irregular
illegitimate	illegitimate	illegitimate	illegitimate	illegitimate
illimitable	illimitable	illimitable	illimitable	illimitable
certain	certain	certain	certain	certain
consider	consider	consider	consider	consider

marked

Total /10

Practice Sheet

Term 1 Set 2 Week 6

Name .... Date 02/11/23

Spelling patterns the prefixes **il-, im-, ir-, extension**, word list

> I can't <u>continue</u> with the <u>impossible</u> demands school makes upon my time!

Spellings	Write	Write	Cover and write	Cover and write	
logical	logical	logical	logical	logical	✓
illogical	illogical	illogical	illogical	illogical	✓
possible	possible	possible	possible	possible	✓
impossible	impossible	impossible	impossible	impossible	✓
responsible	responsible	responsible	responsible	responsible	✓
irresponsible	irresponsible	irresponsible	irresponsible	irresponsible	✓
irrational	irrational	irrational	irrational	irrational	✓
irrefutable	irrefutable	irrefutable	irrefutable	irrefutable	✓
continue	continue	continue	continue	continue	✓
different	different	different	different	different	✓

Total 10 /10

Practice Sheet

Term 1 Set 2 Week 7

Name .... Date ....

Spelling patterns the prefixes **il-, im-, ir-, extension**, word list

Experience has told me that the things we learn at school are not irrelevant.

Spellings	Write	Write	Cover and write	Cover and write
legible	legible	legible	legible	legible
illegible	illegible	illegible	illegible	illegible
patient	patient	patient	patient	patient
impatient	impatient	impatient	impatient	impatient
relevant	relevant	relevant	relevant	relevant
irrelevant	irrelevant	irrelevant	irrelevant	irrelevant
improbable	improbable	improbable	improbable	improbable
imprecise	imprecise	imprecise	imprecise	imprecise
eighth	eight	eight	eight	eight
experience	experience	experience	experience	experience

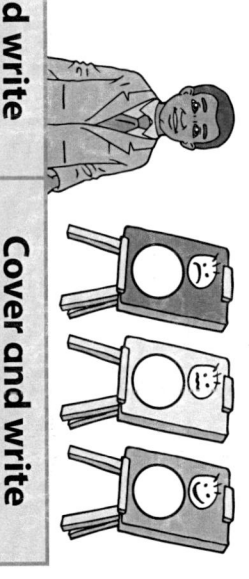

Total 10 /10

11.11.23

Practice Sheet

Term 1 Set 2 Week 8

Name .... Date ....

Spelling patterns the prefixes **il-**, **im-**, **ir-**, **extension**, word list

> I might have been impolite, but slapping me on the face was rather extreme, wasn't it?

Spellings	Write	Write	Cover and write	Cover and write
literate ✓	literate	literate	literate	literate ✓
illiterate ✓	illiterate	illiterate	illiterate	illiterate ✓
polite ✓	polite	polite	polite	polite ✓
impolite ✓	impolite	impolite	impolite	impolite ✓
replaceable ✓	replaceable	replaceable	replaceable	replaceable ✓
irreplaceable ✓	irreplaceable	irreplaceable	irreplaceable	irreplaceable ✓
immovable ✓	immovable	immovable	immovable	immovable ✓
immortal ✓	immortal	immortal	immortal	immortal ✓
experiment ✓	experiment	experiment	experiment	experiment ✓
extreme ✓	extreme	extreme	extreme	extreme ✓

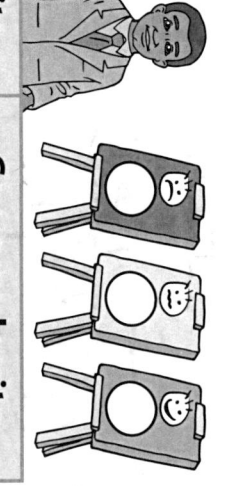

Total 10 /10

Practice Sheet

Term 1 Set 3 Week 9

Name .... Date ....

Spelling patterns the prefixes **sub-**, **inter-**, **anti-**, **auto-**, the suffix **-ation**, **extension**, word list

For your inform<u>ation</u>, I'll be signing <u>auto</u>graphs at the end of the match.

Spellings	Write	Write	Cover and write	Cover and write
subway	subway ✓	subway ✓	subway ✓	subway ✓
intercity	intercity ✓	intercity ✓	intercity ✓	intercity ✓
anticlockwise	anticlockwise ✓	anticlockwise ✓	anticlockwise ✓	anticlockwise ✓
autograph	autograph ✓	autograph ✓	autograph ✓	autograph ✓
inform**ation**	information ✓	information ✓	information ✓	information ✓
admir**ation**	admiration ✓	admiration ✓	admiration ✓	admiration ✓
subdivide	subdivide ✓	subdivide ✓	subdivide ✓	subdivide ✓
antihero	antihero ✓	antihero ✓	antihero ✓	antihero ✓
favourite	favourite ✓	favourite ✓	favourite ✓	favourite ✓
guard	guard ✓	guard ✓	guard ✓	guard ✓

Total 10 /10

SPELLING YEAR 4

© Copyright HeadStart Primary Ltd

Practice Sheet

Term 1 Set 3 Week 10

Name .... Date ....

Spelling patterns the prefixes **sub-**, **inter-**, **anti-**, **auto-**, the suffix **-ation**, **extension**, word list

The new girl wouldn't join in the convers<u>ation</u>, but I soon got her inter<u>acting</u> with other children.

Spellings	Write	Write	Cover and write	Cover and write
submarine	submarine ✓	submarine ✓	submarine ✓	submarine ✓
interact	interact ✓	interact ✓	interact ✓	interact ✓
antiseptic	antiseptic ✓	antiseptic ✓	antiseptic ✓	antiseptic ✓
autobiography	autobiography ✓	autobiography ✓	autobiography ✓	autobiography ✓
adoration	adoration ✓	adoration ✓	adoration ✓	adoration ✓
convers**ation**	conversation ✓	conversation ✓	conversation ✓	conversation ✓
interrelated	interrelated ✓	interrelated ✓	interrelated ✓	interrelated ✓
anticlimax	anticlimax ✓	anticlimax ✓	anticlimax ✓	anticlimax ✓
guide	guide ✓	guide ✓	guide ✓	guide ✓
height	height ✓	height ✓	height ✓	height ✓

Total 10 /10

Practice Sheet

Term 1 Set 3 Week 11

Name .... Date ....

Spelling patterns the prefixes **sub-**, **inter-**, **anti-**, **auto-**, the suffix **-ation**, **extension**, word list

Can you imagine the sensation I caused by hitting four 'sixes' in a row?

Spellings	Write	Write	Cover and write	Cover and write
✓ subheading	subheading	subheading	subheading	subheading
✓ international	international	international	international	international
✓ antisocial	antisocial	antisocial	antisocial	antisocial
✓ automobile	automobile	automobile	automobile	automobile
✓ sensation	sensation	sensation	sensation	sensation
✓ imagination	imagination	imagination	imagination	imagination
✓ intervene	intervene	intervene	intervene	intervene
✓ autopilot	autopilot	autopilot	autopilot	autopilot
✓ imagine	imagine	imagine	imagine	imagine
✓ increase	increase	increase	increase	increase

Total 10 /10

Practice Sheet

Term 1 Set 3 Week 12

Name .... Date ....

Spelling patterns the prefixes **sub-**, **inter-**, **anti-**, **auto-**, the suffix **-ation**, **extension**, word list

My uncle has no <u>knowledge</u> or interest in cars, and put <u>antifreeze</u> in the fuel tank.

Spellings	Write	Write	Cover and write	Cover and write
submerge	submerge	submerge	submerge	submerge ✓
interchange	interchange	interchange	interchange	interchange ✓
antifreeze	antifreeze	antifreeze	antifreeze	antifreeze ✓
automatic	automatic	automatic	automatic	automatic ✓
preparation	preparation	preparation	preparation	preparation ✓
organisation	organisation	organisation	organisation	organisation ✓
confrontation	confrontation	confrontation	confrontation	confrontation ✓
temptation	temptation	temptation	temptation	temptation ✓
interest	interest	interest	interest	interest ✓
knowledge	knowledge	knowledge	knowledge	knowledge ✓

✓ 13.1.24

Total 10 /10

HeadStart
primary

SPELLING • YEAR 4

Practice Sheet

Term 2 Set 1 Week 1

Name .... Date ....

Spelling patterns the suffixes **-ally, -ous, extension,** word list

> Basically Sir, I try to get away with the most outrageous haircuts.

Spellings	Write	Write	Cover and write	Cover and write
basically ✓	basically	basically	basically	basically ✓
humour ✓	humour	humour	humour	humour ✓
humorous ✓	humorous	humorous	humorous	humorous ✓
outrageous ✓	outrageous	outrageous	outrageous	outrageous ✓
various ✓	various	various	various	various ✓
hideous ✓	hideous	hideous	hideous	hideous ✓
truly ✓	truly	truly	truly	truly ✓
automatically ✓	automatically	automatically	automatically	automatically ✓
length ✓	length	length	length	length ✓
library ✓	library	library	library	library ✓

✓ 13·1·14

Total 10 /10

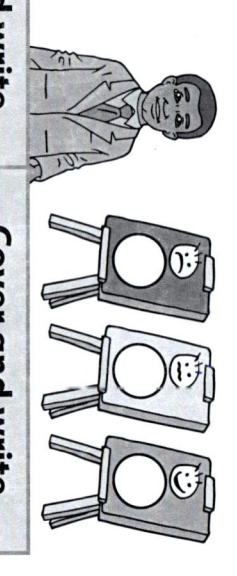

Practice Sheet

Term 2 Set 1 Week 2

Name .... Date ....

Spelling patterns the suffixes **-ally, -ous, extension**, word list

I believe it's better to be natural than try to look glamorous.

Spellings	Write	Write	Cover and write	Cover and write
frantically	frantically ✓	frantically ✓	frantically ✓	frantically ✓
glamour	glamour ✓	glamour ✓	glamour ✓	glamour ✓
glamorous	glamorous ✗	glamorous ✓	glamorous ✓	glamorous ✓
courageous	courageous ✓	courageous ✓	courageous ✓	courageous ✓
serious	serious ✓	serious ✓	serious ✓	serious ✓
spontaneous	spontaneous ✓	spontaneous ✓	spontaneous ✓	spontaneous ✓
duly	duly ✓	duly ✓	duly ✓	duly ✓
publicly	publicly ✓	publicly ✓	publicly ✓	publicly ✓
medicine	medicine ✓	medicine ✓	medicine ✓	medicine ✓
natural	natural ✓	natural ✓	natural ✓	natural ✓

Total 9 /10

Practice Sheet

Term 2 Set 1 Week 3

Name .... Date ....

Spelling patterns the suffixes **-ally, -ous, extension**, word list

> On occasion, I raise my voice dramatically to get the children's attention.

Spellings	Write	Write	Cover and write	Cover and write
dramatically	dramatically	dramatically	dramatically	dramatically ✓
vigour	vigour	vigour	vigour	vigour ✓
vigorous	vigorous	vigorous	vigorous	vigorous ✓
advantageous	advantageous	advantageous	advantageous	advantageous ✓
curious	curious	curious	curious	curious ✓
courteous	courteous	courteous	courteous	courteous ✓
wholly	wholly	wholly	wholly	wholly ✓
gorgeous	gorgeous	gorgeous	gorgeous	gorgeous ✓
occasion	occasion	occasion	occasion	occasion ✓
occasionally	occasionally	occasionally	occasionally	occasionally ✓

Total 10/10

Practice Sheet

Term 2 Set 1 Week 4

Name .... Date ....

Spelling patterns the suffixes **-ally, -ous, extension,** word list

Isn't that odorous smell obvious?

Spellings	Write	Write	Cover and write	Cover and write
historically	historically	historically	historically	historically
odour	odour	odour	odour	odour
odorous	odorous	odorous	odorous	odorous
disadvantageous	disadvantageous	disadvantageous	disadvantageous	disadvantageous
obvious	obvious	obvious	obvious	obvious
instantaneous	instantaneous	instantaneous	instantaneous	instantaneous
drastically	drastically	drastically	drastically	drastically
nauseous	nauseous	nauseous	nauseous	nauseous
notice	notice	notice	notice	notice
opposite	opposite	opposite	opposite	opposite

Total 10 /10

Practice Sheet

Term 2 Set 2 Week 5

Name .... Date ....

Spelling patterns -tion, -ssion, extension, word list

You will have noticed I'm no ordinary singer for I sing with great expression.

Spellings	Write	Write	Cover and write	Cover and write
affection	affection ✓	affection	affection	affection
completion	completion ✓	completion	completion	completion
pollution	pollution ✓	pollution	pollution	pollution
expression	expression ✓	expression	expression	expression
permit	permit ✓	permit	permit	permit
permission	permission ✓	permission	permission	permission
direction	direction ✓	direction	direction	direction
obsession	obsession ✓	obsession	obsession	obsession
ordinary	ordinary ✓	ordinary	ordinary	ordinary
particular	particular ✓	particular	particular	particular

Total 10 /10

SPELLING YEAR 4

© Copyright HeadStart Primary Ltd

Practice Sheet

Term 2 Set 2 Week 6

Name .... Date ....

Spelling patterns -tion, -ssion, extension, word list

Sir, I have a terrible admission: I couldn't do the calculation.

Spellings	Write	Write	Cover and write	Cover and write
exhibition	exhibition	exhibition	exhibition	exhibition
operation	operation	operation	operation	operation
calculation	calculation	calculation	calculation	calculation
discussion	discussion	discussion	discussion	discussion
admit	admit	admit	admit	admit
admission	admission	admission	admission	admission
construction	construction	construction	construction	construction
transmission	transmission	transmission	transmission	transmission
peculiar	peculiar	peculiar	peculiar	peculiar
position	position	position	position	position

Total 10/10

Practice Sheet

Term 2 Set 2 Week 7

Name .... Date ....

Spelling patterns -tion, -ssion, extension, word list

"No *pressure* Sir, but this is an emergency *situation*."

Spellings	Write	Write	Cover and write	Cover and write
correction	correction	correction	correction	correction
relation	relation	relation	relation	relation
situation	situation	situation	situation	situation
confession	confession	confession	confession	confession
omit	omit	omit	omit	omit
omission	omission	omission	omission	omission
celebration	celebration	celebration	celebration	celebration
progression	progression	progression	progression	progression
possession	possession	possession	possession	possession
pressure	pressure	pressure	pressure	pressure

Total 10 /10

Practice Sheet

Term 2 Set 2 Week 8

Name .... Date ....

Spelling patterns -tion, -ssion, extension, word list

I think Mr Stamen gave me the hardest subtrac<u>tion</u> to do on <u>purpose</u>.

Spellings	Write	Write	Cover and write	Cover and write
subtraction	subtraction	subtraction	subtraction	subtraction ✓
translation	translation	translation	translation	translation ✓
hesitation	hesitation	hesitation	hesitation	hesitation ✓
impression	impression	impression	impression	impression ✓
submit	submit	submit	submit	submit ✓
submission	submission	submission	submission	submission ✓
concentration	concentration	concentration	concentration	concentration ✓
profession	profession	profession	profession	profession ✓
probably	probably	probably	probably	probably ✓
purpose	purpose	purpose	purpose	purpose ✓

Total 10 /10

Practice Sheet

Term 2 Set 3 Week 9

Name .... Date ....

Spelling patterns **-sion, -cian, extension**, word list

As an able mathema<u>tician</u>, I'm sure you will want to do all the exten<u>sion</u> work, Blossom.

Spellings	Write	Write	Cover and write	Cover and write
tense				
tension				
extend				
extension				
musician				
mathematician				
diet				
dietician				
recent				
regular				

Total　/10

Practice Sheet

Term 2 Set 3 Week 10

Name .... Date ....

Spelling patterns -sion, -cian, extension, word list

I'm no electrician, but if we don't separate the wires we'll blow the robot's fuse.

Spellings	Write	Write	Cover and write	Cover and write
fuse	fuse	fuse	fuse	fuse
fusion	fusion	fusion	fusion	fusion
expand	expand	expand	expand	expand
expansion	expansion	expansion	expansion	expansion
electrician	electrician	electrician	electrician	electrician
optician	optician	optician	optician	optician
beauty	beauty	beauty	beauty	beauty
beautician	beautician	beautician	beautician	beautician
reign	reign	reign	reign	reign
separate	separate	separate	separate	separate

Total 10 /10

Practice Sheet

Term 2 Set 3 Week 11

Name .... Date ....

Spelling patterns -sion, -cian, extension, word list

This morning's lessons have been torture: grammar revision and a comprehension exercise!

Spellings	Write	Write	Cover and write	Cover and write
revise	revise	revise	revise	revise	✓
revision	revision	revision	revision	revision	✓
comprehend	comprehend	comprehend	comprehend	comprehend	✓
comprehension	comprehension	comprehension	comprehension	comprehension	✓
magician	magician	magician	magician	magician	✓
technician	technical	technical	technical	technical	✓
apprehend	apprehend	apprehend	apprehend	apprehend	✓
apprehension	apprehension	apprehension	apprehension	apprehension	✓
specially	specially	specially	specially	specially	✓
straight	straight	straight	straight	straight	✓

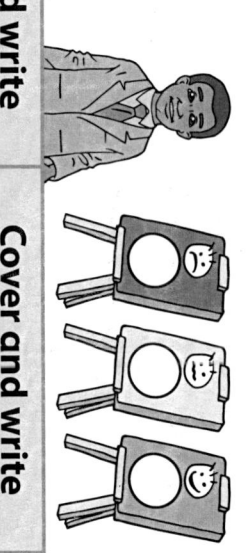

Total 10 /10

SPELLING YEAR 4

© Copyright HeadStart Primary Ltd

Practice Sheet

Term 2 Set 3 Week 12

Name .... Date ....

Spelling patterns **-sion**, **-cian**, extension, word list

I suppose my explanation has left everbody in a state of total confusion.

Spellings	Write	Write	Cover and write	Cover and write
confuse	confuse	confuse	confuse	confuse
confusion	confusion	confusion	confusion	confusion
suspend	suspend	suspend	suspend	suspend
suspension	suspension	suspension	suspension	suspension
politician	politician	politician	politician	politician
physician	physician	physician	physician	physician
supervise	supervise	supervise	supervise	supervise
super**vision**	supervision	supervision	supervision	supervision
strength	strength	strength	strength	strength
suppose	suppose	suppose	suppose	suppose

Total 10 /10

HeadStart
primary

SPELLING • YEAR 4

Practice Sheet

Term 3 Set 1 Week 1

Name .... Date ....

Spelling patterns **ei(gh)**, **ey**, **-gue**, **-que**, **sc** (s sound), **extension**, word list

I'm <u>through</u> with wanting to be a <u>sc</u>ientist.

Spellings	Write	Write	Cover and write	Cover and write
veil	veil	veil	veil	veil
neigh	neigh	neigh	neigh	neigh
survey	survey	survey	survey	survey
league	league	league	league	league
unique	unique	unique	unique	unique
scientist	scientist	scientist	scientist	scientist
catalogue	catalogue	catalogue	catalogue	catalogue
adolescent	adolescent	adolescent	adolescent	adolescent
therefore	therefore	therefore	therefore	therefore
through	through	through	through	through

Total 10 /10

Practice Sheet

Term 3 Set 1 Week 2

Name .... Date ....

Spelling patterns **ei(gh)**, **ey**, **-gue**, **-que**, **sc** (s sound), **extension**, word list

> And here we have an antique mobile phone, probably dating back to the eighteen hundreds.

Spellings	Write	Write	Cover and write	Cover and write
beige	beige	beige	beige	beige
eighteen	eighteen	eighteen	eighteen	eighteen
surveyor	surveyor	surveyor	surveyor	surveyor
pla**gue**	plague	plague	plague	plague
antique	antique	antique	antique	antique
scenery	scenery	scenery	scenery	scenery
colleague	colleague	colleague	colleague	colleague
iso**sc**eles	isosceles	isosceles	isosceles	isosceles
though	though	though	though	though
although	although	although	although	although

Total 9/10

Practice Sheet

Term 3 Set 1 Week 3

Name .... Date ....

Spelling patterns ei(gh), ey, -gue, -que, sc (s sound), extension, word list

Just a <u>thought</u>, Sir, but would a sizeable <u>cheque</u> get me a good report?

Spellings	Write	Write	Cover and write	Cover and write
reign	reign	reign	reign	reign ✓
sleigh	sleigh	sleigh	sleigh	sleigh ✓
convey	convey	convey	convey	convey ✓
rogue	rogue	rogue	rogue	rogue ✓
cheque	cheque	cheque	cheque	cheque ✓
discipline	discipline	discipline	discipline	discipline ✓
grotesque	grotesque	grotesque	grotesque	grotesque ✓
disciple	disciple	disciple	disciple	disciple ✓
thought	thought	thought	thought	thought ✓
various	various	various	various	various ✓

Total 10 /10

Practice Sheet

Term 3 Set 1 Week 4

Name .... Date ....

Spelling patterns **ei(gh)**, **ey**, **-gue**, **-que**, **sc** (s sound), **extension**, word list

> Some people say my ton**gue** is the most overworked mu**sc**le in my body.

Spellings	Write	Cover and write	Cover and write
sheikh	sheikh	sheikh	sheikh ✓
n**eigh**bour	neighbour	neighbour	neighbour ✓
conv**ey**or	conveyor	conveyor	conveyor ✓
ton**gue**	tongue	tongue	tongue ✓
mos**que**	mosque	mosque	mosque ✓
mu**sc**le	muscle	muscle	muscle ✓
pla**que**	plaque	plaque	plaque ✓
fa**sc**inate	fascinate	fascinate	fascinate ✓
variety	variety	variety	variety ✓
w**eigh**t	weight	weight	weight ✓

Total 10 /10

Practice Sheet

Term 3 Set 2 Week 5

Name .... Date ....

Spelling patterns **ch** (k sound), **ch** (sh sound), **homophones** and **near-homophones**, extension

I have a cunning scheme to avoid choir practice.

Spellings	Write	Write	Cover and write	Cover and write
scheme	scheme	scheme	scheme	scheme ✓
choir	choir	choir	choir	choir ✓
chalet	chalet	chalet	chalet	chalet ✓
chic	chic	chic	chic	chic ✓
knot	knot	knot	knot	knot ✓
not	not	not	not	not ✓
missed	missed	missed	missed	missed ✓
mist	mist	mist	mist	mist ✓
monarch	monarch	monarch	monarch	monarch ✓
chauffeur	chauffeur	chauffeur	chauffeur	chauffeur ✓

Total 10 /10

Practice Sheet

Term 3 Set 2 Week 6

Name .... Date ....

Spelling patterns **ch** (k sound), **ch** (sh sound), **homophones** and **near-homophones**, extension

After eating four hot dogs, a burger and five doughnuts, I've got a stomach ache.

Spellings	Write	Write	Cover and write	Cover and write
ache	ache	ache	ache	ache
stomach	stomach	stomach	stomach	stomach
parachute	parachute	parachute	parachute	parachute
charade	charade	charade	charade	charade
mail	mail	mail	mail	mail
male	male	male	male	male
wood	wood	wood	wood	wood
would	would	would	would	would
architect	architect	architect	architect	architect
chandelier	chandelier	chandelier	chandelier	chandelier

Total ...... /10

SPELLING YEAR 4

© Copyright HeadStart Primary Ltd

Practice Sheet

Term 3 Set 2 Week 7

Name .... Date ....

Spelling patterns **ch** (k sound), **ch** (sh sound), **homophones** and **near-homophones**, extension

> You can have a plain old cheese and onion pie, or my fabulous quiche Lorraine.

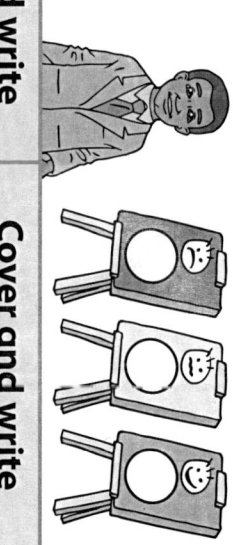

Spellings	Write	Write	Cover and write	Cover and write
chemist	chemist	chemist	chemist	chemist
chaos	chaos	chaos	chaos	chaos
champagne	champagne	champagne	champagne	champagne
quiche	quiche	quiche	quiche	quiche
main	main	main	main	main
mane	mane	mane	mane	mane
plain	plain	plain	plain	plain
plane	plane	plane	plane	plane
orchestra	orchestra	orchestra	orchestra	orchestra
chivalry	chivalry	chivalry	chivalry	chivalry

Total 10 /10

Practice Sheet

Term 3 Set 2 Week 8

Name .... Date ....

Spelling patterns **ch** (k sound), **ch** (sh sound), **homophones** and **near-homophones**, extension

> It's important that I wear a false moustache in this scene.

Spellings	Write	Write	Cover and write	Cover and write
echo	echo	echo	echo	echo
mechanic	mechanic	mechanic	mechanic	mechanic
moustache	moustache	moustache	moustache	moustache
machete	machete	machete	machete	machete
medal	medal	medal	medal	medal
meddle	meddle	meddle	meddle	meddle
scene	scene	scene	scene	scene
seen	seen	seen	seen	seen
technology	technology	technology	technology	technology
fuchsia	fuchsia	fuchsia	fuchsia	fuchsia

Total 10 /10

Practice Sheet

Term 3 Set 3 Week 9

Name .... Date ....

Spelling patterns homophones and near-homophones

It might be summer, but in this country we have to <u>accept</u> whatever <u>weather</u> we get.

Spellings	Write	Write	Cover and write	Cover and write
accept	accept	accept	accept	accept
except	except	except	except	except
whether	whether	whether	whether	whether
weather	weather	weather	weather	weather
whose	whose	whose	whose	whose
who's	who's	who's	who's	who's
air	air	air	air	air
heir	heir	heir	heir	heir
sight	sight	sight	sight	sight
site	site	site	site	site

Total /10

Practice Sheet

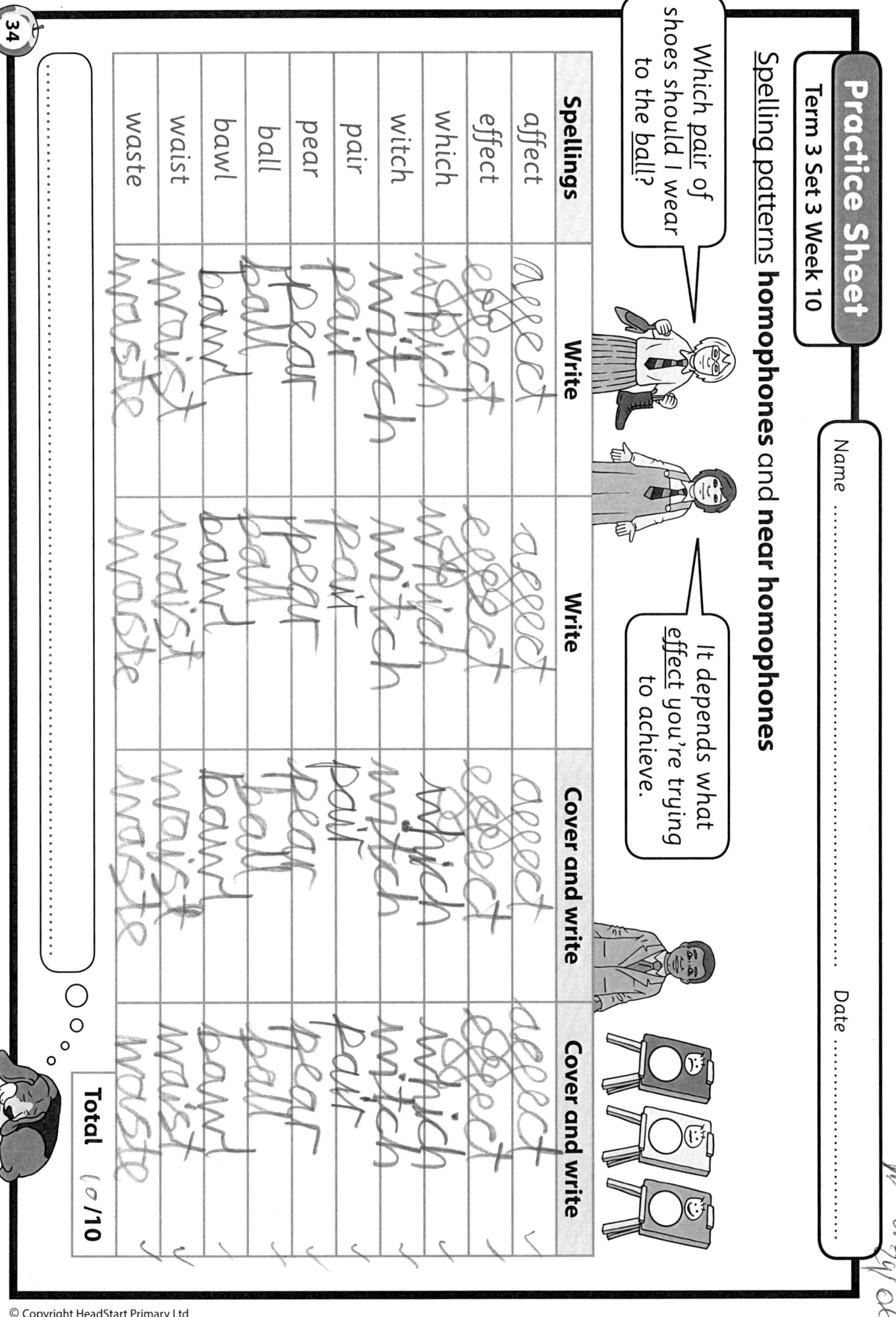

Term 3 Set 3 Week 10

Name .... Date ....

Spelling patterns **homophones** and **near homophones**

> Which <u>pair</u> of shoes should I wear to the <u>ball</u>?

> It depends what <u>effect</u> you're trying to achieve.

Spellings	Write	Write	Cover and write	Cover and write
affect	affect	affect	affect	affect
effect	effect	effect	effect	effect
which	which	which	which	which
witch	witch	witch	witch	witch
pair	pair	pair	pair	pair
pear	pear	pear	pear	pear
ball	ball	ball	ball	ball
bawl	bawl	bawl	bawl	bawl
waist	waist	waist	waist	waist
waste	waste	waste	waste	waste

Total 10 /10

Practice Sheet

Term 3 Set 3 Week 11

Name .... Date ....

Spelling patterns homophones and near homophones

> My dad has grown a great hairy beard, and now he looks like Mr Twit.

Spellings	Write	Write	Cover and write	Cover and write
brake	brake	brake	brake	brake
break	break	break	break	break
fair	fair	fair	fair	fair
fare	fare	fare	fare	fare
grate	grate	grate	grate	grate
great	great	great	great	great
groan	groan	groan	groan	groan
grown	grown	grown	grown	grown
berry	berry	berry	berry	berry
bury	bury	bury	bury	bury

Total 10 /10

HeadStart
primary

ACTIVITY SHEETS
Term 1

SPELLING • YEAR 4

© Copyright HeadStart Primary Ltd

Activity Sheet
Term 1 Set 1 Week 1

Name ....

For most words of **two syllables** that have the stress on the last syllable, you need to **double the last letter** when you add a **suffix**.

Add the suffix -ed, -ing, -er or -en to the following words. Don't forget to double the last consonant.

✓ regret **ted**   ✓ regret **ting**
✓ commit **ted**   ✓ commit **ting**
✓ begin **ner**   ✓ begin **ning**
✓ admit **ted**   ✓ admit **ting**
✓ refer **red**   ✓ refer **ring**
✓ prefer **red**   ✓ prefer **ring**
✓ forgot **ten**   ✓ forget **ting**
✓ forbid **den**   ✓ forbid **ding**

Complete the words in the sentences below.

✓ I'm begin **ning** to enjoy myself.

✓ I'm surprised you're admit **ting** that!

✓ I've forgot **en** what to do!

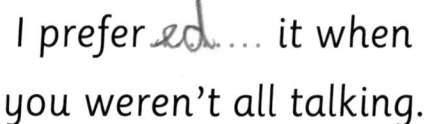

✓ I prefer **ed** it when you weren't all talking.

36

SPELLING YEAR 4

Activity Sheet
Term 1 Set 1 Week 1

Name ....

> For words of **two syllables** where the last syllable is unstressed, you **don't double** the last consonant.

Add the suffix *-ed*, *-ing*, *-er* or *-en* to the following words.

limit ed   limit ing
fidget ed   fidget ing
fasten ed   fasten ing
happen ed   happen ing
offer ed   offer ing
benefit ed   benefit ing
budget ed   budget ing
target ed   target ing

Complete the words in the sentences below.

What's happened to my pencil?

I offered my pencil, but you wouldn't take it.

I benefited from listening carefully.

Would you please stop fidgeting?

checked

Activity Sheet
Term 1 Set 1 Week 2

Name ....

> When adding suffixes, some **two syllables** words need the final consonant **doubling**. It depends where the stress lies.

Add -ing to the words below.

commit ✓   limit ✓   fasten ✓   regret ✓   admit ✓   happen ✓
offer ✓   forget ✓ prefer ✓   target ✓   begin ✓   fidget ✓

> I'm collecting all words that need the final consonant doubling.

> I'm collecting all words that **don't** need the final consonant doubling.

✓ admitting
✓ forgetting
✓ committing
✓ regretting
✓ beginning
✓ preferring
✓ happenning

limiting ✓
fidgeting ✓
targeting ✓
offering ✓
fastening ✓

Complete the words in the sentences below.

> I'm begin**ning** ✓ to regret forget**ting** ✓ my PE kit. Petal offer**ed** to lend me her pumps, but I much prefer**red** ✓ Twiggy's pumps.

38

SPELLING YEAR 4

Activity Sheet
Term 1 Set 1 Week 2

Name ....

Match the words in the box to the children's definitions.

| accidentally | actually | believe | bicycle |
| breathe | business | caught | century |

The past tense of catch is ..caught..... ✓

A vehicle that you pedal is called a ..bicycle..... ✓

A job or a profession is sometimes called a ..business.. ✓

Something done by mistake is done ..accidentally..

A hundred years make a ..century..... ✓

To accept that something is true is to ..believe..... ✓

When we take air into the lungs we ..breathe..... ✓

We can replace the word really with ..actually..

✓ marked

SPELLING YEAR 4

Activity Sheet
Term 1 Set 1 Week 3

Name ....

Use the spellings below to complete the sentences.

accidentally ✓   actually ✓   believe ✓   bicycle ✓
breathe ✓   business ✓   caught ✓   century ✓

Sprout _actually_ ✓ expected me to _believe_ ✓ his silly story!

I got _caught_ ✓ on the boundary just as I was about to make my _century_ ✓.

It's none of your _business_ ✓ what I decide to do.

I _accidentally_ ✓ added the sums instead of taking away!

My sister has just learnt to ride her _bicycle_ ✓ without stabilisers.

I could hardly _breate_ ✗ (breathe ✓) after completing the cross-country race.

40

SPELLING YEAR 4

Activity Sheet
Term 1 Set 1 Week 3

Name ....

Use the words below to complete the sentences.

committing ✓   visiting ✓   admitted ✓   limited ✓
beginning ✓   regretted ✓   happened ✓   fidgeting ✓

Sprout *admitted* that he was the one who hid Petal's pencil case.

Our local MP will be *visiting* the school.

My knowledge of French is very *limited*, but I am willing to learn.

I *regretted* telling you my secret.

Mr Stamen thinks that *fidgeting* in class is *committing* a crime.

Tell me what *happened* again and this time start at the *beginning*.

✓ marked

SPELLING YEAR 4

Activity Sheet
Term 1 Set 1 Week 4

Name ....

Write your own sentences using the words in the boxes.

offered

✓ I offered him a piece of chocolate.

beginning

✓ I got the toilet at the beginning of assembly.

limited

✓ I get a limited amount of time to watch TV.

referred

✓ The question referred to maths.

regretted

✓ I regretted wasting my money on a dress.

fastened

✓ I fastened my seat belt in the car.

admitting

✓ I saw him admitting his mistake.

committed

✓ He committed a big crime.

SPELLING YEAR 4

Activity Sheet
Term 1 Set 1 Week 4

Name ....

Spud's Spelling Bingo

You will need a partner to play this game. Below is a list of the words you have been learning from Set 1.

regretted	committing	referred	admitted	forbidden
fidgeting	fastened	offered	limited	targeted
budgeted	forgotten	bicycle	actually	believe
accidentally	breathe	business	caught	century

Choose nine words and write them in the grid below.
(Your partner will write nine words in their grid.)

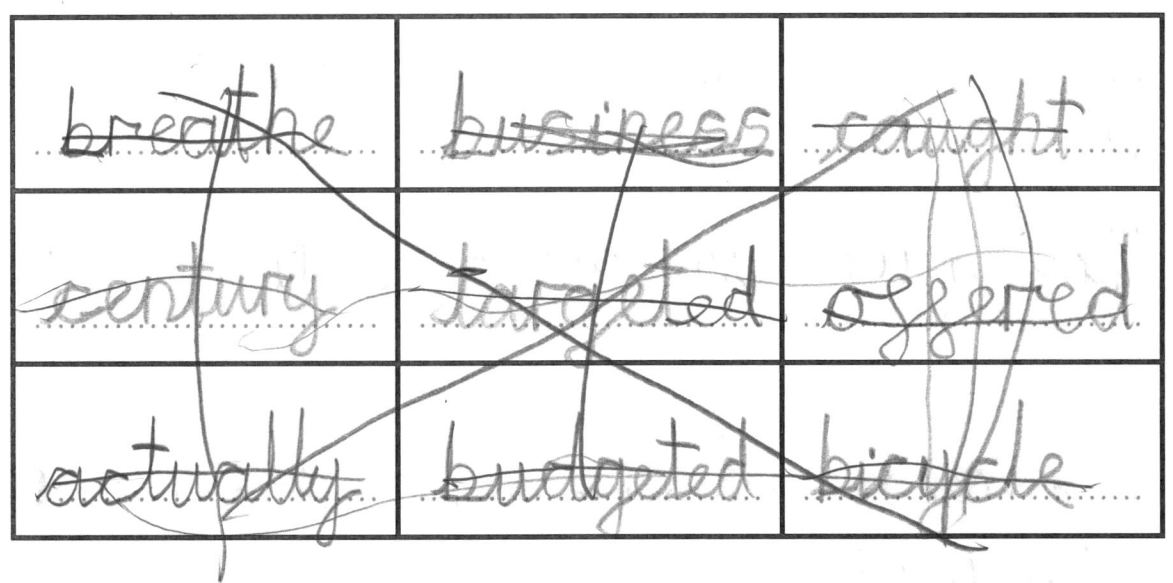

breathe	business	caught
century	targeted	offered
actually	budgeted	bicycle

Now try to guess which words your partner has written in their grid. Take it in turns. Remember to cross out the words you have said, so that you don't repeat them.

You get:

1 point for the first horizontal line.

1 point for the first vertical line.

1 point for the first diagonal line.

3 points for a full house.

Now test each other on the words in the grid. (Don't peek!)

You get **1 point** for each correct spelling. Who's got the most points?

SPELLING YEAR 4

Activity Sheet
Term 1 Set 2 Week 5

Name ....

You can give some words the opposite meaning by adding a prefix.

Add **il-** to my words.

Add **im-** to my words.

Add **ir-** to my words.

✓ **il**legal
✓ **il**logical
✓ **il**legible
✓ **il**literate
✓ **il**legitimate
✓ **il**limitable

immature
✓ **im**possible
✓ **im**patient
✓ **im**polite
✓ **im**probable
✓ **im**precise

✓ **ir**regular
✓ **ir**responsible
✓ **ir**relevant
✓ **ir**replaceable
✓ **ir**rational
✓ **ir**refutable

Complete the sentences below using the words above.

✓ You can be very **impatient** at times!

✓ Oops! Sorry! That was very **immature** of me!

✓ That is very **impolite** behaviour.

✓ You've made me laugh so much my writing is **imprecise**.

44

SPELLING YEAR 4

Activity Sheet
Term 1 Set 2 Week 5

Name ....

Add the prefix *il-*, *im-* or *ir-* to the following words to give the words the opposite meaning.

- ✓ **il**logical
- ✓ **im**mature
- ✓ **ir**replaceable
- ✓ **im**possible
- ✓ **ir**rational
- ✓ **il**literate
- ✓ **im**patient
- ✓ **ir**regular
- ✓ **im**probable
- ✓ **im**precise
- ✓ **im**movable
- ✓ **ir**relevant
- ✓ **ir**responsible
- ✓ **im**mortal
- ✓ **il**legal
- ✓ **il**legible
- ✓ **im**polite
- ✓ **ir**refutable

Complete the words in the sentences below.

✓ What's an **ir**regular triangle?

✓ I think it's an **im**precisely drawn triangle.

✓ Perhaps it's an **il**legal triangle!

✓ Those answers are all highly **im**probable.

✓ marked

45

SPELLING YEAR 4

Activity Sheet
Term 1 Set 2 Week 6

Name ....

Add the correct prefixes to the words below.

~~legible~~   ~~patient~~   ~~replaceable~~   ~~mature~~   ~~literate~~   ~~rational~~
~~possible~~   legitimate   ~~regular~~   responsible   ~~polite~~   ~~legal~~
~~relevant~~   ~~logical~~   ~~probable~~   ~~refutable~~   ~~precise~~   limitable

I'm collecting all words that use the prefix **il-**.

I'm collecting all words that use the prefix **im-**.

I'm collecting all words that use the prefix **ir-**.

il-	im-	ir-
illegible	impatient	irreplaceable
illiterate	immature	irrational
illegitimate	impossible	irregular
illegal	impolite	irresponsible
illogical	improbable	irrelevant
illimitable	imprecise	irrefutable

Add the correct prefix to the words in the speech bubble.

Don't be **im**patient, children. You must not act in an **ir**rational or **ir**responsible manner. It is **il**logical to come to that conclusion based on the facts.

SPELLING YEAR 4

Activity Sheet
Term 1 Set 2 Week 6

Name ....

Match the words in the box to the children's definitions.

| ~~certain~~ | ~~consider~~ | ~~continue~~ | ~~different~~ |
| ~~eighth~~ | ~~experience~~ | ~~experiment~~ | ~~extreme~~ |

Knowledge and skill gained with practice is *experience*.

The opposite of the word same is *different*.

To carry on is to *continue*.

One of eight equal parts is an *eighth*.

To think carefully is to *consider*.

A scientific investigation is called an *experiment*.

Very large in amount or degree is *extreme*.

When you are sure, you are *certain*.

47

SPELLING YEAR 4

© Copyright HeadStart Primary Ltd

Activity Sheet
Term 1 Set 2 Week 7

Name ....

Use the spellings below to complete the sentences.

~~certain~~   ~~consider~~   ~~continue~~   ~~different~~
~~eighth~~   ~~experience~~   experiment   ~~extreme~~

I'm *certain* that the letter 'h' is the *eighth* letter of the alphabet.

You should *consider* your answer before you *continue* your work.

Bean doesn't have enough *experience* to be on the school council.

I'm going to try a *different* method for solving the problem.

Sprout can be an *extreme* pain at times!

Will my *experiment* to create a new life form work?

SPELLING YEAR 4

Activity Sheet
Term 1 Set 2 Week 7

Name ....

Use the words below to complete the sentences.

irregular   impolite   illegible   immature
irrelevant   impatient   irresponsible   impossible

"Wait a minute! You are so **impatient** at times, Sprout."

"None of its sides are the same, so it is an **irregular** triangle."

"You are displaying very **immature** and **irresponsible** behaviour."

"This writing is **illegible**. It is **impossible** to read."

"It's **impolite** to point at people."

"The answer you have given to my question is **irrelevant**."

SPELLING YEAR 4

Activity Sheet
Term 1 Set 2 Week 8

Name ....

Write your own sentences using the words in the boxes.

illegal

✓ Killing a person is illegal.

illiterate

✓ The boy in my class is illiterate.

illogical

✓ The maths equation was illogical.

irreplaceable

✓ The Crown Jewels are irreplaceable.

continue

✓ I will continue to do my work.

certain

✓ I'm certain that the answer to the question is wrong.

experiment

✓ That chemistry experiment is interesting.

different

✓ This animal is part of a different species.

SPELLING YEAR 4

Activity Sheet
Term 1 Set 2 Week 8

Name ....

Spud's Spelling Bingo

You will need a partner to play this game. Below is a list of the words you have been learning from Set 3.

~~illegal~~   illogical   ~~illegible~~   ~~illiterate~~   ~~immature~~
impossible   ~~impatient~~   ~~impolite~~   irregular   irresponsible
~~irrelevant~~   irreplaceable   ~~certain~~   ~~continue~~   consider
~~different~~   ~~eighth~~   ~~experiment~~   ~~experience~~   ~~extreme~~

Choose nine words and write them in the grid below.
(Your partner will write nine words in their grid.)

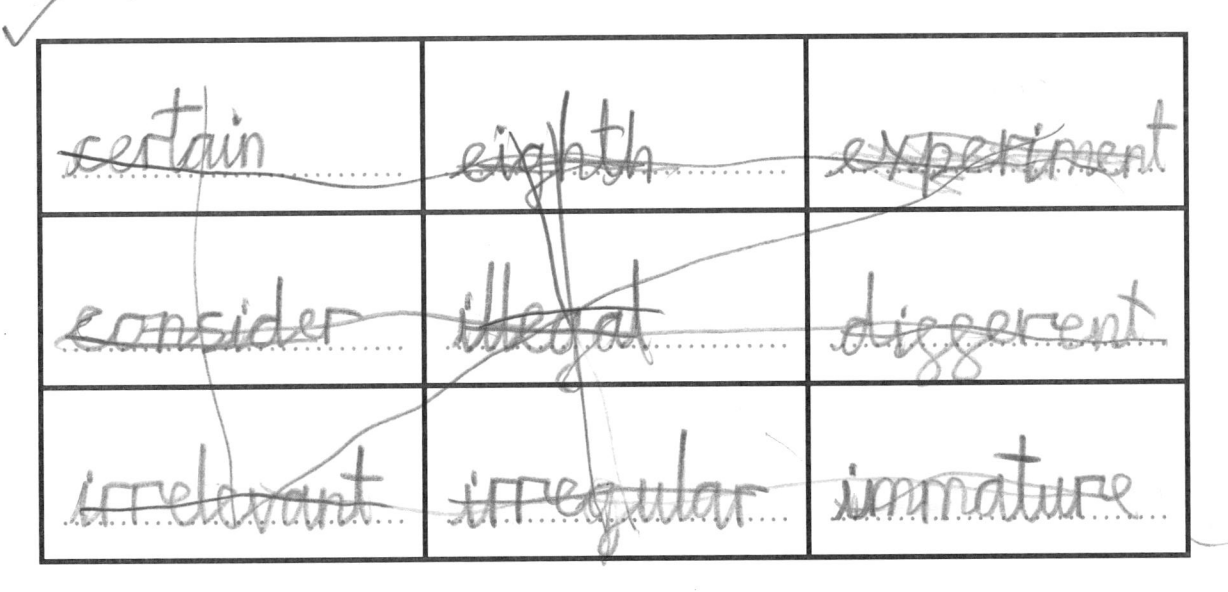

certain	eighth	experiment
consider	illegal	different
irrelevant	irregular	immature

Now try to guess which words your partner has written in their grid. Take it in turns. Remember to cross out the words you have said, so that you don't repeat them.

You get:

1 point for the first horizontal line.

1 point for the first vertical line.

1 point for the first diagonal line.

3 points for a full house.

Now test each other on the words in the grid. (Don't peek!)

You get **1 point** for each correct spelling. Who's got the most points?

SPELLING YEAR 4

11·18

Activity Sheet
Term 1 Set 3 Week 9

Name ....

Prefixes can change the meaning of the base word.

Add **sub-** to my words.

✓ **sub**way
✓ **sub**marine
✓ **sub**heading
✓ **sub**merge
✓ **sub**divide

Add **inter-** to my words.

✓ **inter**city
✓ **inter**act
✓ **inter**national
✓ **inter**change
✓ **inter**related

Add **anti-** to my words.

✓ **anti**clockwise
✓ **anti**septic
✓ **anti**social
✓ **anti**freeze
✓ **anti**hero

Add **auto-** to my words.

✓ **auto**graph
✓ **auto**biography
✓ **auto**mobile
✓ **auto**matic
✓ **auto**pilot

SPELLING YEAR 4

Activity Sheet
Term 1 Set 3 Week 9

Name ....

Add the prefix *sub-*, *inter-*, *anti-* or *auto-* to complete the words in the following sentences.

I turned *anti*...clockwise to face west.

We walked through the *sub*...way to get to the other side of the road.

I have Harry Kane's *auto*... graph.

We caught the *inter*...city train to London Euston.

You need to write a *sub*...heading under the headline.

English has become an *inter*...national language.

In America they call cars *auto*...mobiles.

Come and play with us. Don't be *anti*...social.

SPELLING YEAR 4

Activity Sheet
Term 1 Set 3 Week 10

Name ....

Add the suffix *-ation* to the words in brackets in the sentences below to make new words. Words ending in *e* need the *e* taking off before adding the suffix.

✓ I believe you have some top secret ....*information*.... (inform) for me.

✓ Thank you, Mr Stamen. I've really enjoyed our little ....*conversation*.... (converse).

✓ Come on, Sprout. You've got to try to use more ....*imagination*.... (imagine).

✓ This chicken and mushroom pie is a taste ....*sensation*.... (sense).

✓ We shall have to form a mutual ....*admiration*.... (admire) society.

✓ Winning the Spelling Bee took weeks of mental ....*preparation*.... (prepare).

SPELLING YEAR 4

Activity Sheet
Term 1 Set 3 Week 10

Name ....

Match the words in the box to the children's definitions.

| favourite ✓ | guard ✓ | guide ✓ | height ✓ |
| imaglne ✓ | increase ✓ | interest ✓ | knowledge ✓ |

The vertical measurement of something is *height*.

To make greater in size or amount is to *increase*.

The thing you prefer the most is your *favourite*.

Imagine is to form a mental picture in your head.

To watch over and protect is to *guard*.

Understanding facts and information is *knowledge*.

A person who shows the way to others is a *guide*.

The feeling of wanting to know more about something is an *interest*.

SPELLING YEAR 4

Activity Sheet
Term 1 Set 3 Week 11

Name ....

Use the spellings in the box to complete the sentences.

| favourite | guard | guide | height |
| imagine | increase | interest | knowledge |

If you read this book, it will help to _increase_ your _knowledge_.

I _imagine_ football is your _favourite_ sport.

After football, my second favourite _interest_ is food.

Spud will _guard_ his bone all day.

We are both about the same _height_.

Spud makes a terrific _guide_ dog!

SPELLING YEAR 4

Activity Sheet
Term 1 Set 3 Week 11

Name ....

Use the words below to complete the sentences.

~~subway~~ ~~interact~~ ~~automobiles~~ ~~imagination~~
~~submerge~~ ~~intercity~~ ~~antisocial~~ ~~autograph~~
~~information~~ submarine subheading ~~antifreeze~~

I **interact** with all the children because I am not **antisocial**.

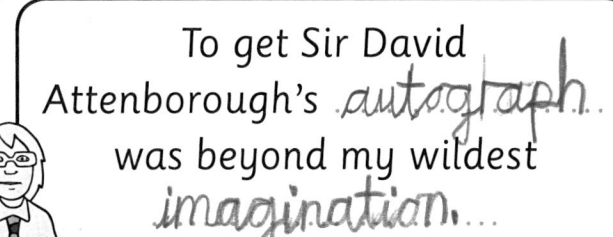

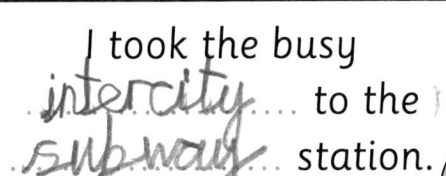

To get Sir David Attenborough's **autograph** was beyond my wildest **imagination**.

I took the busy **intercity** to the **subway** station.

A nuclear **submarine** can **submerge** to a depth of 490 metres.

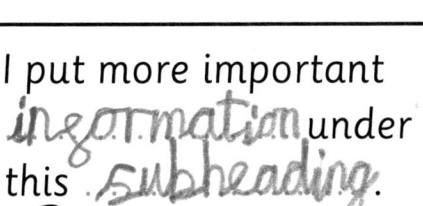

I put more important **information** under this **subheading**.

It can get very cold in America, so they have to make sure there is plenty of **antifreeze** in their **automobile**.

SPELLING YEAR 4

Activity Sheet
Term 1 Set 3 Week 12

Name ....

What do you think the children would say if they had to use the words in the boxes?

autobiography — I wrote my autobiography.

sensation — The beach is a sensation.

admiration — I have admiration for Ed Sheeran.

interact — I can interact with people online.

antiseptic — After I got hurt, my teacher applied antiseptic on me.

submerge — The submarine is going to submerge into the water.

SPELLING YEAR 4

Activity Sheet
Term 1 Set 3 Week 12

Name ....

Spud's Word Finder Game

You will need a partner to play this game. Below is a list of the words you have been learning from Set 1.

subway	submarine	subheading	submerge	subdivide
intercity	interact	international	interchange	intervene
antisocial	antiseptic	anticlockwise	antifreeze	antihero
autograph	autobiography	automobile	automatic	autopilot
information	preparation	conversation	imagination	guard
favourite	organisation	height	interest	knowledge

✓ **Choose a word and write it in one of the boxes below. Your partner will do the same.**

There are three boxes so you can play the game up to three times. However, you can also play it on a piece of paper or a mini whiteboard.

....	....	....

✓ **The object of the game is to find out which letters are in the word in your partner's box and guess what the word is.**

Take it in turns to ask your partner if the word contains a letter of your choice. Put the correct letters in Spud's bowl. The first person to guess the word is the winner. You can guess the word at any point during the game, but only before your turn. However, if you guess wrong, Spud goes in the doghouse and you are out of the game.

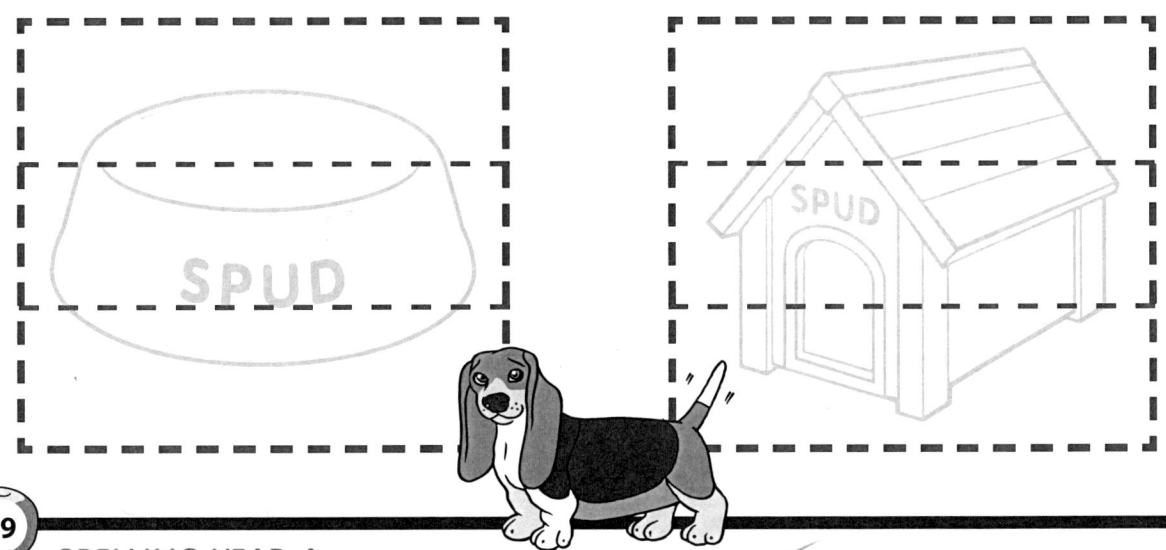

SPELLING YEAR 4

13·1·24

HeadStart
primary

ACTIVITY SHEETS

Term 2

SPELLING • YEAR 4

© Copyright HeadStart Primary Ltd

Activity Sheet
Term 2 Set 1 Week 1

Name ....

Add suffixes to the words below.

If the word ends in c, add the suffix -ally.

basic	**basically**
frantic	*frantically* ✓
dramatic	*dramatically* ✓
historic	*historically* ✓
automatic	*automatically* ✓

If adding -ous to words ending in -our, change to -or.

humour	**humorous**
glamour	*glamorous* ✓
vigour	*vigorous* ✓
odour	*odorous* ✓
rigour	*rigorous* ✓

If adding -ous to words ending in -ge, keep the e.

outrage	**outrageous**
courage	*courageous* ✓
advantage	*advantage* ✓
disadvantage	*disadvantage* ✓
rampage	*rampage* ✓

SPELLING YEAR 4

Activity Sheet
Term 2 Set 1 Week 1

Name ....

Usually the *i* sound before *-ous* is spelt with an *i*, but sometimes it is spelt with an *e*.

Which word in the groups below is the odd one out?

The odd one out is *hideous* ✓ .

various   studious   hideous   previous   hilarious

The odd one out is *spontaneous* ✓ .

serious   notorious   envious   spontaneous   victorious

The odd one out is *courteous* ✓ .

curious   obvious   glorious   rebellious   courteous

Four words below have been misspelt. Circle the spelling mistakes and correct them.

victorious   curious   spontaneous   obvious   (gloreous)
rebellious   (courtious)   studious   (hidious)   previous
hilarious   (sereous)   notorious   various   envious

Corrections   ✓ serious   ✓ hideous
              ✓ glorious   ✓ courteous

SPELLING YEAR 4

✓ 13.1.24

Activity Sheet
Term 2 Set 1 Week 2

Name ....

Add the suffix *-ous* to the words in the brackets in the sentences below to make new words. Don't forget that some changes will be necessary.

Sprout is always doing funny things. He is a very _humorous_ (humour) boy.

It's _outrageous_ (outrage) that we are being made to stay in!

Vigorous (vigour) exercise makes you sweat!

Mr Stamen said I was a very _courageous_ (courage) person standing up to that bully.

I want to look _glamorous_ (glamour) for my birthday party.

It would be _advantageous_ (advantage) to speak to Mr Stamen about the extra playtime when he is in a good mood.

SPELLING YEAR 4

Activity Sheet
Term 2 Set 1 Week 2

Name ....

Match the words in the box to the children's definitions.

| length | library | medicine | natural |
| occasion | occasionally | notice | opposite |

A drug for the treatment of disease is *medicine*.

To see or pay attention to something is to *notice*.

A building where books are kept is a *library*.

Something that is situated on the other side is *opposite*.

The measurement of the longest sides is the *length*.

A particular event can be called an *occasion*.

Anything not artificially made by man is *natural*.

When something happens now and then we say it happens *occasionally*.

SPELLING YEAR 4

Activity Sheet
Term 2 Set 1 Week 3

Name ....

Use the spellings in the box to complete the sentences.

| length | library | medicine | natural |
| occasion | occasionally | notice | opposite |

Occasionally, I need to take *medicine* for my asthma.

How did you not *notice* that Sprout was standing *opposite* you?

Mr Stamen sent me out to measure the *length* of the football pitch.

The *library* is my favourite room in the school.

Cats are Spud's *natural* enemy.

Mr Stamen is wearing a suit. Is it some special *occasion*?

SPELLING YEAR 4

Activity Sheet
Term 2 Set 1 Week 3

Name ....

Use the words below to complete the sentences.

~~dramatically~~ ~~obvious~~ ~~basically~~ ~~glamorous~~
~~historically~~ ~~advantageous~~ ~~serious~~ ~~odorous~~
~~humorous~~ ~~instantaneous~~ ~~hideous~~ ~~vigorous~~

The *glamorous* actress *dramatically* exited the stage.

It was *obvious* to me that the film about Elizabeth I was *historically* inaccurate.

Sprout can never be *serious*. Everything is *humorous* to him.

Mr Stamen said it was *advantageous* for our health to do *vigorous* exercise.

The *hideous* creature of the swamp crawled out of the *odorous* bog.

Basically, the match was won due to my *instantaneous* reactions.

SPELLING YEAR 4

Activity Sheet
Term 2 Set 1 Week 4

Name ....

What do you think the children would say if they had to use the words in the boxes?

frantically — She shouted frantically at Jill.

various — I had various number of choises to make.

curious — I was curious about what would happen next in the book.

courteous — Joel was a courteous man.

outrageous — I get outrageous when someone annoys me.

courageous — I'm a courageous boy.

✓ VA

SPELLING YEAR 4

Activity Sheet
Term 2 Set 1 Week 4

Name ....

Spud's Word Finder Game

You will need a partner to play this game. Below is a list of the words you have been learning from Set 1.

basically	frantically	dramatically	historically	drastically
humour	glamour	vigour	rigour	odour
humorous	glamorous	vigorous	rigorous	odorous
outrageous	courageous	advantageous		various
hideous	serious	curious		obvious
disadvantageous	spontaneous	courteous	instantaneous
length	library	medicine	occasion	opposite

Choose a word and write it in one of the boxes below. Your partner will do the same.

There are three boxes so you can play the game up to three times. However, you can also play it on a piece of paper or a mini whiteboard.

The object of the game is to find out which letters are in the word in your partner's box and guess what the word is.

Take it in turns to ask your partner if the word contains a letter of your choice. Put the correct letters in Spud's bowl. The first person to guess the word is the winner. You can guess the word at any point during the game, but only before your turn. However, if you guess wrong, Spud goes in the doghouse and you are out of the game.

SPELLING YEAR 4

Activity Sheet
Term 2 Set 2 Week 5

Name ....

Add the suffix -ion to the words below.

Add -ion to my words. No change to the root word is necessary.

Add -ion to my words. You will need to remove the e before adding the suffix.

affect	**affection**	complete	**completion**
exhibit ✓	exhibition	operate ✓	operation
correct ✓	correction	pollute ✓	pollution
subtract ✓	subtraction	calculate ✓	calculation
direct ✓	direction	hesitate	hesitation

Add -ion to my words. No change is necessary.

Add -ion to my words. Change the t to ss before adding the suffix.

express	**expression**	permit	**permission**
discuss ✓	discussion	admit ✓	admission
confess ✓	confession	omit ✓	omission
impress ✓	impression	submit ✓	submission
obsess ✓	obsession	transmit ✓	transmission

SPELLING YEAR 4

Activity Sheet
Term 2 Set 2 Week 5

Name ....

Add the suffix *-ion* to the words below. Remember: sometimes you have to make changes to the root word.

Affect becomes

✓ *affection*

Hesitate becomes

✓ *hesitation*

Progress becomes

✓ *progression*

Admit becomes

✓ *admission*

Impress becomes

✓ *impression*

Correct becomes

✓ *corection*

Permit becomes

✓ *permition*

Pollute becomes

✓ *pollution*

Relate becomes

✓ *relation*

Omit becomes

✓ *omission*

SPELLING YEAR 4

Activity Sheet
Term 2 Set 2 Week 6

Name ....

Add the suffix *-ion* to the words in the brackets to complete the sentences.
Don't forget to make any changes necessary.

I went to an art _exhibition_ (exhibit) at the weekend.

It left me with a very good _impression_ (impress).

There is a lot of _pollution_ (pollute) in our cities.

The _situation_ (situate) isn't good for the environment.

You can't come to the disco without your _admission_ (admit) ticket.

Perhaps Mr Stamen will give you _permission_ (permit) to come in.

Did you do the _correction_ (correct) for maths?

It was a very hard _calculation_ (calculate).

SPELLING YEAR 4

Activity Sheet
Term 2 Set 2 Week 6

Name ....

Match the words in the box to the children's definitions.

| ordinary | particular | peculiar | position |
| possession | pressure | probably | purpose |

Something that is owned is a *possession*.

When you push very hard against something, you exert *pressure*.

Something that is odd or strange is *peculiar*.

Normal means the same as *ordinary*.

The reason for doing something is the *purpose*.

The location of something is its *position*.

Almost certainly is the same as *probably*.

We use the word *particular* when it is related to a single person or thing.

71
SPELLING YEAR 4

Activity Sheet
Term 2 Set 2 Week 7

Name ....

Use the words in the box below to complete the sentences.

ordinary   particular   peculiar   position
possession   pressure   probably   purpose

I hope you didn't do that on ...purpose...

I think I was absent on that ...paticular... day.

This dictionary is my most prized ...possesion.... I am certainly no ...ordinary... student.

This milk has a ...peculiar... taste. It's ...probably... gone off.

You're putting me under so much ...pressure... to get it right!

I'm not in a ...position... to answer that question.

72

SPELLING YEAR 4

Activity Sheet
Term 2 Set 2 Week 7

Name ....

Use the words below to complete the sentences.

impression ✓   discussion ✓   permission ✓   affection ✓
pollution ✓   translation ✓   hesitation ✓   subtraction ✓
exhibition ✓   completion ✓   calculation ✓   relation ✓

There wasn't a moment's **hesitation** as Mr Stamen completed the **subtraction**.

Mr Stamen gave us the **impression** that the **exhibition** of our work was a great success.

We had a class **discussion** about the **pollution** that's causing global warming.

I was happy at the **completion** of the French **translation** I did for homework.

I have great **affection** for my very good friend and **relation**.

I asked Mr Stamen for **permission** not to do the hard **calculation** sum.

SPELLING YEAR 4

Activity Sheet
Term 2 Set 2 Week 8

Name ....

What do you think the children would say if they had to use the words in the boxes?

> I get a weird impression on him sometimes

impression

> ....

omission

> Today was my earliest homework submission

submission

> There is a very bad situation going on

situation

> I had a really good expression about that poem.

expression

> He has a confession to make.

confession

SPELLING YEAR 4

Activity Sheet
Term 2 Set 2 Week 8

Name ....

Spud's Spelling Bingo

You will need a partner to play this game. Below is a list of the words you have been learning from Set 2.

affection	exhibition	~~correction~~	~~subtraction~~	~~completion~~
~~relation~~	~~calculation~~	~~situation~~	hesitation	pollution
~~expression~~	~~discussion~~	confession	impression	~~progression~~
~~permission~~	~~admission~~	omission	~~submission~~	transmission
ordinary	~~particular~~	possession	probably	purpose

Choose nine words and write them in the grid below.
(Your partner will write nine words in their grid.)

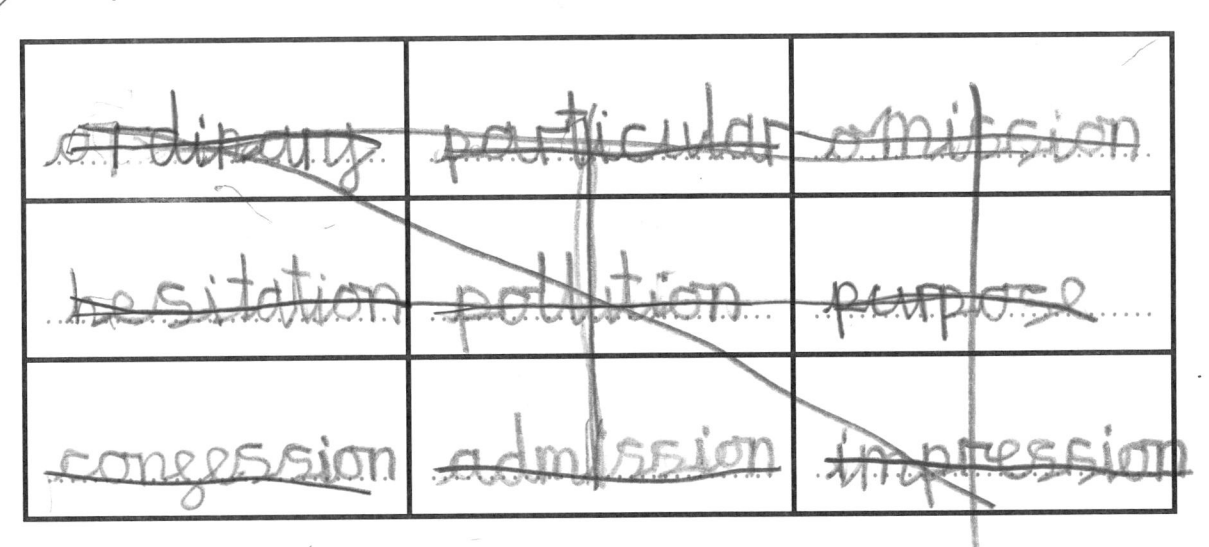

ordinary	particular	omission
hesitation	pollution	purpose
confession	admission	impression

Now try to guess which words your partner has written in their grid. Take it in turns. Remember to cross out the words you have said, so that you don't repeat them.

You get:

1 point for the first horizontal line.

1 point for the first vertical line.

1 point for the first diagonal line.

3 points for a full house.

Now test each other on the words in the grid. (Don't peek!)

You get **1 point** for each correct spelling. Who's got the most points?

SPELLING YEAR 4

Activity Sheet
Term 2 Set 3 Week 9

Name ....

Add the suffix -ion to the words below.

Add **-ion** to my words. You will need to remove the **e** before adding the suffix.

Add **-ion** to my words. You will need to change the **d** to an **s** before adding the suffix.

tense	**tension**	extend	**extension**
fuse	....	expand	....
revise	....	comprehend	....
confuse	....	suspend	....
supervise	....	apprehend	....

Some words sound like they have the ending **-sion**, but they are spelt **-cian**. This is the case for words that end in **c** or **cs**.

Add **-ian** to my set of words.

music	**musician**
electric	....
optic	....
magic	....
technic	....
politics	....

76

SPELLING YEAR 4

Activity Sheet
Term 2 Set 3 Week 9

Name ....

Add the ending -ion to the words below. Remember: sometimes you have to make changes to the root word.

Fuse becomes
....

Expand becomes
....

Tense becomes
....

Extend becomes
....

Comprehend becomes
....

Revise becomes
....

Confuse becomes
....

Suspend becomes
....

Supervise becomes
....

Apprehend becomes
....

SPELLING YEAR 4   INCOMPLETE

Activity Sheet
Term 2 Set 3 Week 10

Name ....

Add the ending -ian to the words in the brackets to complete the sentences.
Don't forget to make any changes necessary.

I would love to be a *mathematician* (mathematics). ✓

I love playing my violin, so I could also be a *musician* (music). ✓

My dad is an *electrician* (electric). ✓

But I think I would rather be a *magician* (magic). ✓

I got my glasses at the *optician* (optic). ✓

A dental *technician* (technic) made my nan's dentures. ✓

Elizabeth Garrett Anderson was Britain's first female *physician* (physics). ✓

I either want to be a doctor or a *politician* (politics). ✓

78

SPELLING YEAR 4

Activity Sheet
Term 2 Set 3 Week 10

Name ....

Match the words in the box to the children's definitions.

| recent ✓ | regular | reign | separate ✓ |
| specially ✓ | straight ✓ | strength | suppose ✓ |

To rule as the king or queen is to *reign* ✓.

When you are physically strong, you have *strength* ✓.

If something always happens at the same time, we say it is *regular* ✓.

When you think something is true, but you are not sure you *suppose* ✓.

When something happened not long ago it is *recent* ✓.

If something is without a curve or a bend, then it is *straight* ✓.

When something is done for a particular reason, we say it is done *specially* ✓.

When something is apart from other things, we say it is *seperate* ✓.

SPELLING YEAR 4

Activity Sheet
Term 2 Set 3 Week 11

Name ....

Use the words in the box below to complete the sentences.

recent	regular	reign	separate
specially	straight	strength	suppose

I ..suppose.. you would all like an extra ten minutes playtime.

In order to build up your ..strength.., you need to train on a ..regular.. basis.

In ..recent.. weeks, I have been Star of the Week on three ..separate.. occasions.

I couldn't keep a ..straight.. face after Sprout fell off his chair.

I made this ..specially.. for you!

Queen Victoria's ..reign.. lasted for nearly sixty-four years.

SPELLING YEAR 4

Activity Sheet
Term 2 Set 3 Week 11

Name ....

Use the words below to complete the sentences.

~~tension~~   confusion   ~~musician~~   ~~extension~~
technician   ~~apprehension~~   ~~mathematician~~   fusion
expansion   politician   supervision   ~~comprehension~~

For those of you who want to do it, there is an *extension* task in the *comprehension* exercise.

There was a feeling of *apprehension* and *tension* before the cup match.

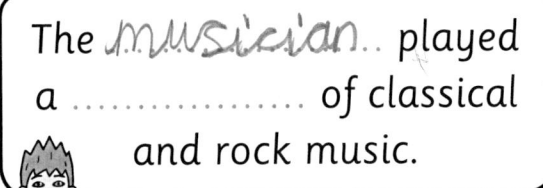

The *musician* played a .... of classical and rock music.

The *mathematician* said that algebra was important for the .... of our brains.

The speech by our local .... just led to more ....

Our computer .... said we couldn't work on the laptops without ....

81

SPELLING YEAR 4

Activity Sheet
Term 2 Set 3 Week 12

Name ....

What do you think the children would say if they had to use the words in the boxes?

The revision of a subject is really important.

revision

I was in a state of congusion when he told his story.

confusion

"He did a good joke at being a musician!" I said.

musician

The suspesion ear the car wasn't good.

suspension

He was a wonderful magician.

magician

I went to the optician to get my eyes checked.

optician

SPELLING YEAR 4

Activity Sheet
Term 2 Set 3 Week 12

Name ....

Spud's Spelling Scrabble

Below is a list of the words you have been learning from Set 3.

tension	fusion	revision	~~confusion~~	supervision
extension	expansion	~~comprehension~~	suspension	apprehension
musician	~~electrician~~	~~mathematician~~	magician	politician
optician	physician	recent	reign	regular
separate	specially	straight	strength	suppose

How many words can you make from the twelve letters below. You can use the letters twice. Try to fill the grid.

| s | i | e | t | r | u | o | n | p | a | v | x |

physician	regular	opticial
tension	specially	apprehension
magician	recent	musician

SPELLING YEAR 4

HeadStart primary

ACTIVITY SHEETS
Term 3

SPELLING • YEAR 4

© Copyright HeadStart Primary Ltd

Activity Sheet
Term 3 Set 1 Week 1

Name ....

Words that sound like they are spelt *ay* are sometimes spelt *ei*, *eigh* or *ey*.

neigh   beige   convey   sheikh
surveyor   veil   sleigh   conveyor
neighbour   reign   eighteen   survey

I'm collecting all **ei** words.

I'm collecting all **eigh** words.

I'm collecting all **ey** words.

beige   sleigh   surveyor
veil   reign   convey
reign   neighbour   conveyor
sheikh   eighteen   survey

Some words sound like they end in **g**, but are spelt **gue**.
Some words sound like they end in **k**, but are spelt **que**.

Add **-gue** to my set of words.

Add **-que** to my set of words.

lea.gue   anti.que
pla.gue   uni.que
ro.gue   che.que
ton.gue   mos.que

SPELLING YEAR 4

Activity Sheet
Term 3 Set 1 Week 1

Name ....

Some words have the *s* sound, but are spelt *sc*. Put *sc* into the words below to complete them, then match them to their dictionary definition.

scientist — training people to obey rules

scenery — a young person who is developing from a child into an adult

di**sc**ipline — a follower of Jesus

mu**sc**le — **someone who has expert knowledge about natural or physical sciences**

adole**sc**ent — the tissue in a human or animal body that produces movement

iso**sc**eles — the natural features of a landscape

di**sc**iple — to attract strong attention and interest

fa**sc**inate — a triangle with two sides of equal length

SPELLING YEAR 4

Activity Sheet
Term 3 Set 1 Week 2

Name ....

Use the words in the box to complete the sentences below.

rogue	conveyor	reigning	league
eighteen	cheque	tongue	antique

I'm the _reigning_ champion and top goal scorer.

I am in a _league_ of my own!

You're a cheeky _rogue_, young man.

Don't poke your _tongue_ out at me.

My dad bought an old picture from an _antique_ shop.

The _cheque_ was made out for two hundred pounds.

The food went along the _conveyor_ belt to the checkout operator.

My mum had to pay _eighteen_ pounds for the shopping.

SPELLING YEAR 4

Activity Sheet
Term 3 Set 1 Week 2

Name ....

Use the words in the box to complete the sentences below.

| therefore ✓ | through ✓ | though ✓ | although ✓ |
| thought ✓ | various ✓ | variety ✓ | weight ✓ |

I ...*thought*... that exercise was very difficult.

You are a school councillor now and ...*therefore*... have responsibilities.

The school hall is used for ...*various*... purposes.

I think Mr Stamen has put on a bit of ...*weight*... .

I have a lot of work to get ...*through*... today.

Even ...*though*... the plate was piled high, I ate only three cookies.

I'm very knowledgeable on a ...*variety*... of different topics.

...*Although*... it was raining, we still went out to play.

SPELLING YEAR 4

Activity Sheet
Term 3 Set 1 Week 3

Name ....

Use the words in the box below to complete the sentences in your own words. You don't need to use all eight words.

therefore	through	though	although
thought	various	variety	weight

I was looking _through the window_.

I've eaten so many doughnuts _though I've also eaten lots of fruits_.

I'm glad you said that because _I thought the same_.

I can name several different _varieties of flowers_.

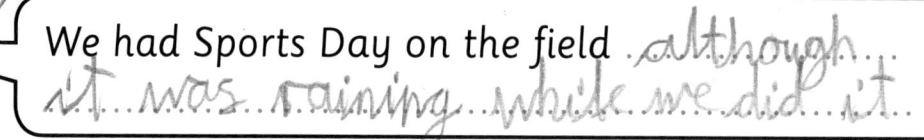

We had Sports Day on the field _although it was raining while we did it_.

Bean came up with _an excellent idea, various options_.

88

SPELLING YEAR 4

Activity Sheet
Term 3 Set 1 Week 3

Name ....

Use the words below to complete the sentences.

~~unique~~   ~~adolescent~~   ~~scientist~~   ~~reigning~~
survey   ~~beige~~   ~~eighteen~~   ~~neighbour~~
~~plague~~   ~~scenery~~   discipline   ~~sheikh~~

Edward III was the **reigning** monarch during the Black **plague**.

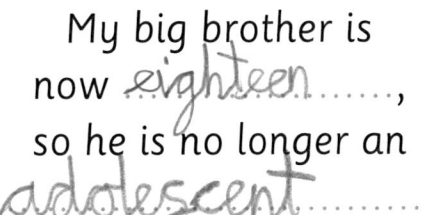

My big brother is now **eighteen**, so he is no longer an **adolescent**.

The **scientist** who came to school told us that everybody's fingerprint is **unique**.

The rich Arab **sheikh** wore a white turban and a **beige** coloured robe.

My next-door **neighbour** said that **discipline** in the local school was good.

From the top of the hill, you can **survey** the beautiful **scenery** below.

SPELLING YEAR 4

Activity Sheet
Term 3 Set 1 Week 4

Name ....

What do you think the children would say if they had to use the words in the boxes?

I'm building up my muscle.

muscles

I wore a veil to the temple.

veil

They did a democracy survey amongst a 1000 people.

survey

"Watch your tongue," I said to Jacob.

tongue

Learn how to discipline yourself.

discipline

Muslims go to the mosque.

mosque

SPELLING YEAR 4

Activity Sheet
Term 3 Set 1 Week 4

Name ....

Spud's Spelling Scrabble

Below is a list of the words you have been learning from Set 1.

veil ✗	beige ✗	~~reign~~	~~sleigh~~	~~eighteen~~
~~neigh~~	survey ✗	surveyor	convey ✗	conveyor ✗
league ✗	plague ✗	rogue	~~tongue~~	catalogue ✗
antique ✗	~~unique~~	cheque ✗	mosque ✗	plaque ✗
scientist ✗	scenery ✗	discipline ✗	muscle ✗	fascinate ✗
~~through~~	~~though~~	~~thought~~	various ✗	variety ✗

How many words can you make from the twelve letters below. You can use the letters twice. Try to fill the grid.

| s | r | l | n | e | t | i | o | g | u | h | q |

✓ eighteen	✓ neigh	✓ through
✓ tongue	✓ unique	though
✓ sleigh	✓ reign	thought

SPELLING YEAR 4

Activity Sheet
Term 3 Set 2 Week 5

Name ....

Words spelt with a *ch* sometimes have a k sound or even a *sh* sound.

scheme	chalet	ache	chemist
chic	choir	charade	chaos
echo	parachute	mechanic	quiche
machete	stomach	champagne	moustache
monarch	orchestra	chauffeur	chandelier

*I'm collecting all **ch** words that sound like they have been spelt with a **k**.*

*I'm collecting all **ch** words that sound like they have been spelt with a **sh**.*

✓ scheme
✓ ache
✓ chemist
✓ choir
✓ chaos
✓ echo
✓ mechanic
✓ stomach
✓ monarch
✓ orchestra

chalet ✓
chic ✓
charade ✓
parachute ✓
quiche ✓
machete ✓
champagne ✓
moustache ✓
chauffeur ✓
chandelier ✓

SPELLING YEAR 4

Activity Sheet
Term 3 Set 2 Week 5

Name ....

> Some words are called **homophones** or **near-homophones**. These are words that sound the same, but are spelt differently and have different meanings.

Write the correct homophone from the brackets to complete the sentences below.

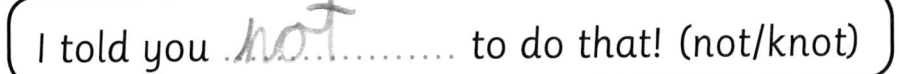

I told you ...*not*... to do that! (not/knot)

I can't believe I ...*missed*... that penalty. (missed/mist)

I got some ...*mail*... in the post. (male/mail)

Has anyone lost a ...*pair*... of pumps? (pear/pair)

I came into school by the ...*main*... entrance. (main/mane)

Could you give me a piece of ...*plain*... paper? (plain/plane)

Please don't ...*meddle*... with my pencils. (medal/meddle)

Have you ...*seen*... the mess you've made? (scene/seen)

SPELLING YEAR 4

Activity Sheet
Term 3 Set 2 Week 6

Name ....

Use the words in the box to complete the sentences below.

| ~~chalet~~ | ~~choir~~ | quiche | ~~ache~~ |
| ~~champagne~~ | chemist | ~~stomach~~ | ~~echo~~ |

Miss Seed is looking for people who want to sing in the school *choir*.

Would you stop repeating everything I say? It sounds like there's an *echo* in the class.

My *stomach* feels really full.

I think I've eaten too much cheese *quiche*.

We're going to stay in a *chalet* in France.

Mum says she's going to eat oysters and drink *champagne*.

I've got a terrible *ache* in my head.

We'll have to go to the *chemist* to get some medicine.

SPELLING YEAR 4

Activity Sheet
Term 3 Set 2 Week 6

Name ....

Use one of the pairs of homophones in the box to complete the sentences below.

plane/plain   see/scene   missed/mist   not/knot
pair/pear   medal/meddle   main/mane   male/mail

I couldn't find my way to school because of the *mist*.

The *plane* had to make an emergency landing.

I won my first *medal* in the school sports day.

We are going to read the *scene* with Aunt Sponge and Aunt Spiker.

I have a ham sandwich and a *pear* in my lunch box today.

The horse was grey with a white *mane* and tail.

The *male* peacock has colourful tail feathers.

Who can undo the *knot* in my shoelaces?

SPELLING YEAR 4

Activity Sheet
Term 3 Set 2 Week 7

Name ....

Use the words in the box below to complete the sentences in your own words. You don't need to use all eight words.

| chaos   scheme   moustache   charades |
| machete   mechanic   parachute   chic |

✓ As it was my party, *we did some charades.*

✗ My dad took our car to the garage where *mechanic objectes were.*

✗ I come back into the classroom and *study.* ??

✓ To raise money for charity, *we sold parachutes.*

✓ He's shaved it off now, but *he had a good looking beard moustache.*

✓ Listen carefully, *Sarah has a crush on Jake.*

SPELLING YEAR 4

Activity Sheet
Term 3 Set 2 Week 7

Name ....

What do you think the children would say if they had to use the words in the boxes?

I like technology.

technology

I've seen an orchestra

orchestra

"My stomach is gully," I said.

stomach

He is my chauggeur

chauffeur

My voice echoed through the halway

echo

I enjoyed the ride on the parachute

parachute

SPELLING YEAR 4

Activity Sheet
Term 3 Set 2 Week 8

Name ....

Spud's Spelling Scrabble

Below is a list of the words you have been learning from Set 2.

scheme ✓	ache	chemist ✓	echo	choir ✓
mechanic ✓	chaos ✓	stomach ✓	monarch	architect
chalet ✓	parachute ✓	champagne ✓	moustache ✓	chic ✓
charade ✓	quiche ✓	machete ✓	chandelier	chivalry
meddle ✓	scene ✓	missed	plain	knot

How many words can you make from the twelve letters below. You can use the letters twice. Try to fill the grid.

| s | a | c | t | h | o | e | l | m | n | k | q |

hole	cat	monk
maths	act	mash
thanks	loathe	lame

98

SPELLING YEAR 4

Activity Sheet
Term 3 Set 2 Week 8

Name ....

Spud's Spelling Search

Find as many words as possible from Set 2. You may use a list to help you.

S	F	Z	D	M	L	F	Y	X	C	C	A	C	R	F
C	T	S	I	M	E	H	C	H	E	I	B	H	A	M
H	E	N	E	C	S	E	A	H	H	N	E	A	E	A
E	E	K	C	T	X	M	C	P	F	A	H	O	P	C
M	M	C	Y	H	P	A	D	A	A	H	C	S	V	H
E	N	C	H	A	I	E	H	R	W	C	A	X	H	E
U	N	E	G	O	S	C	M	A	C	E	T	R	Y	T
R	C	N	E	S	G	I	E	C	M	M	S	J	Q	E
I	E	H	I	S	S	O	D	H	D	H	U	C	A	W
O	W	M	A	T	Q	K	S	U	S	M	O	H	W	J
H	N	Q	I	R	J	U	L	T	E	E	M	A	F	T
C	P	A	I	R	A	M	I	E	V	D	Z	L	C	P
E	L	D	D	E	M	D	K	C	W	A	Y	E	Y	X
S	T	O	M	A	C	H	E	B	H	L	P	T	L	C
O	F	P	F	Z	A	H	X	Q	B	E	J	L	B	X

There are **24 words** from **Set 2** to find. They are set out horizontally, vertically and diagonally. To make it harder, some words read backwards. Write the words as you find them on the lines below.

- stomach
- choir
- scheme
- machete
- meddle
- chic
- chemist
- champagne
- parachute
- moustache
- quiche
- mechanic
- chaos
- chalet
- charade
- scene

SPELLING YEAR 4

Activity Sheet
Term 3 Set 3 Week 9

Name ....

Write the correct homophone from the brackets to complete the sentences below.

Will you .... his apologies? (accept/except)

I don't know .... I should go to the disco or not. (weather/whether)

I'm looking forward to a .... from all this spelling. (brake/break)

Your actions .... his behaviour. (affect/effect)

What .... you do in that situation? (wood/would)

Spud likes to .... his bones. (berry/bury)

Have you got the .... for the bus into town? (fare/fair)

I hate the .... of blood! (site/sight)

SPELLING YEAR 4

Activity Sheet
Term 3 Set 3 Week 9

Name ....

Use one of the pairs of homophones in the box to complete the sentences below.

~~grate/great~~ ~~waste/waist~~ ~~ball/bawl~~ ~~accept/except~~
~~groan/grown~~ ~~which/witch~~ ~~air/heir~~ ~~who's/whose~~

I don't know **which** question I should do first.

We had a **great** time at the summer fair.

I'll have that sausage. Don't let it go to **waste**.

My hair has **grown** too long.

When Blossom fell over and cut herself, she started to **bawl**.

Are you the boy **who's** always making rude noises?

Everybody **except** Sprout can have a piece of cake.

Who is the **heir** to the throne?

SPELLING YEAR 4

Activity Sheet
Term 3 Set 3 Week 10

Name ....

What do you think the children would say if they had to use the words in the boxes?

accept — Always accept your mistake.

except — I will play with everyone except James.

weather — Go and check the weather forcast.

whether — I don't whether I'm going or not.

would — Would is a homophone of wood.

wood — Don't chop down trees for wood.

witch — People refer to witches as being bad.

which — I don't know which option to pick.

SPELLING YEAR 4

Activity Sheet
Term 3 Set 3 Week 10

Name ....

The wrong homophone has been used in the following sentences. Write the correct homophone for the sentence.

Sprout will grown when he knows he has another spelling test. **groan**

Did Bean decide witch book to choose? **which**

I can't decide weather I should play with Petal or Twiggy. **whether**

It's dangerous to play on the building sight. **site**

The back break isn't working on my bike. **brake**

Bean wood like his felt tips back. **would**

Spud berries his bone in the middle of the field. **burries**

Put it in the waist paper basket. **waste**

Will you except this invitation to my party? **accept**

Who's turn is it next? **whose**

Are you going to the summer fare this year? **fair**

Our class assembly was interrupted when a baby started to ball. **bawl**

When Henry VIII died, who was the legitimate air to the throne? **heir**

Our new timetable will come into affect from next week. **effect**

Twiggy scored a really grate goal to win the match. **great**

103

SPELLING YEAR 4

Activity Sheet
Term 3 Set 3 Week 11

Name ....

Match the dictionary definition to the correct homophone.

~~break/brake~~	~~grate/great~~	~~which/witch~~
~~waste/waist~~	~~air/heir~~	~~except/accept~~
~~ball/bawl~~	~~weather/whether~~	~~site/sight~~
fare/fair	~~bury/berry~~	~~grown/groan~~

✓ To smash into pieces .... *break*

✓ To make a low noise usually in pain or despair .... *groan*

✓ The conditions in the atmosphere such as wind, rain and temperature .... *weather*

✓ The part of the human body above the hips .... *waist*

✓ The power of seeing .... *sight*

✓ To reduce food to small shreds .... *grate*

✓ The money paid for a journey on public transport .... *fare*

✓ A small round fruit .... *berry*

✓ A woman thought to have magic power .... *witch*

✓ The invisible gas surrounding the earth .... *air*

✓ To agree to receive something .... *accept*

✓ To shout or cry noisily .... *bawl*

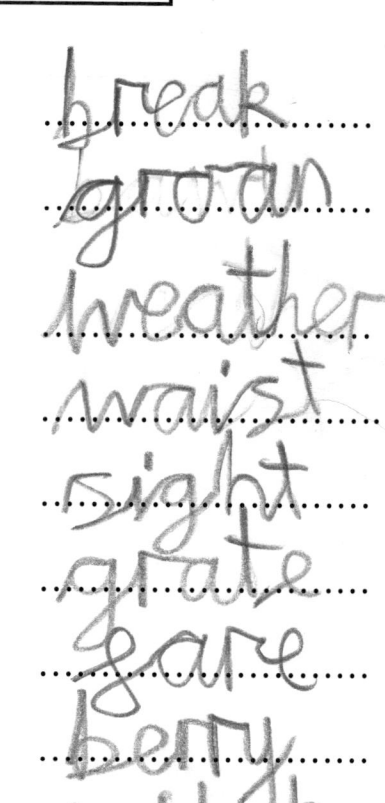

104

SPELLING YEAR 4

Activity Sheet
Term 3 Set 3 Week 11

Name ....

Spud's Spelling Search

Find as many words as possible from Set 3. You may use a list to help you.

W	H	E	T	H	E	R	S	J	W	C	A	S	K	B
G	W	P	D	O	O	W	U	A	I	F	B	D	L	R
I	M	F	A	B	O	J	S	T	E	A	Z	E	W	A
F	D	L	S	E	N	T	N	H	T	C	D	R	Z	M
B	J	I	X	R	E	A	P	G	A	C	W	A	L	Y
J	T	P	T	R	N	K	I	I	R	E	A	F	D	P
E	R	A	T	Y	M	L	K	S	G	P	I	U	Q	E
G	E	W	T	C	E	F	F	A	W	T	S	L	L	S
B	R	S	E	T	E	E	B	H	E	O	T	W	A	Z
R	D	O	A	A	X	F	C	D	Y	R	U	S	E	S
C	I	E	W	C	T	I	F	R	D	Q	B	L	S	M
Z	R	A	E	N	H	H	U	E	A	Q	H	V	D	Z
G	T	P	F	W	M	B	E	W	I	T	C	H	A	I
C	T	G	R	O	A	N	H	R	E	K	A	R	B	F
F	H	P	A	Y	A	T	T	N	H	J	T	A	O	S

There are **24 words** from **Set 3** to find. They are set out horizontally, vertically and diagonally. To make it harder, some words read backwards. Write the words as you find them on the lines below.

- groan
- witch
- whether
- berry
- grown
- waist
- air
- grate
- brake
- break
- fare
- waste
- sight
- bury

SPELLING YEAR 4